365 DAYS OF

positivity

DAILY GUIDANCE
FOR A HAPPIER YOU

summersdale

365 DAYS OF POSITIVITY

Debbi Marco has asserted her right to be identified as the author of this work in accordance with sections 77 and 78 of the Copyright, Designs and Patents Act 1988.

An Hachette UK Company
www.hachette.co.uk

Summersdale Publishers Ltd
Part of Octopus Publishing Group Limited
Carmelite House
50 Victoria Embankment
LONDON
EC4Y 0DZ
UK

www.summersdale.com

Printed and bound in China

ISBN: 978-1-80007-102-5

Substantial discounts on bulk quantities of Summersdale books are available to corporations, professional associations and other organizations. For details contact general enquiries: telephone: +44 (0) 1243 771107 or email: enquiries@summersdale.com.

To ....

From ....

introduction

There is plenty to be positive about in life; you just need to learn how to look properly. This book is here to show you how. Whether your glass is looking half empty or you can't seem to find the silver lining in the clouds, there are plenty of little things you can do each day to help you look on the bright side of life. Feeling happier will have a knock-on effect on all aspects of your life, because once you're in a positive state of mind, you're in a better place to start thinking about your goals. It can even have a beneficial impact on your physical health, your relationships and even your work. Wherever you are in your life, changing your mindset to a more optimistic one can transform your fortunes. Everything is possible with a little

bit of positivity. Think of this book as your own personal cheerleader to help you through the year. Each day has an uplifting quote or helpful, accessible tip as well as ideas for fun activities to help you see the light when life is looking gloomy. Now all you have to do is turn the page and embrace the day!

january

01

Instead of setting a New Year's resolution, step into this year feeling open to all possibilities and unburdened by the fear of failing.

02

Have a kitchen disco. While you're waiting for the kettle to boil take a moment to put on your favourite song and dance. It will boost your endorphins and make you forget any worries for a few minutes.

Let us make our future now, and let us make our dreams tomorrow's reality.

MALALA YOUSAFZAI

Start your day right. It might be tough to get out of bed in the mornings, but instead of hitting the snooze button when your alarm goes off, swing your legs out of bed and plant them on the floor. Breathe deeply — open a window if you can — and embrace the day.

Create a gratitude jar. Every time you feel grateful for something, write it down on a piece of paper and pop it in a jar. Then pull one out whenever you're feeling gloomy.

Get your body moving at the start of every day. Drop your chin to your chest and roll forward until your head and arms are hanging toward the floor. Roll yourself up and repeat.

Give a compliment. Whether someone has done a great job at work or you love their new haircut, let them know. Not only will you make them feel better, but you'll give yourself a boost, too.

Breathe. The previous weeks may have been quite a rollercoaster as you negotiated the holiday season, so take some time to be still. Inhale through your nose for a count of four, hold your breath for a count of four and then exhale for a count of six. Try to do this for a few minutes several times a day.

Take time out to read a magazine. There's something about sinking into a comfy chair and flicking through the pages of a glossy magazine that feels indulgent. You might be inspired by something you see – perhaps you'll see a city you'd like to visit or a recipe you want to make.

Today you're not going to idle on Instagram or fiddle around on Facebook. Log out, delete the apps and discover how much better you feel when you're not lusting over someone else's life.

Set yourself a physical challenge. Start small and work on it every day until you get there. See what you can achieve when you put your mind to something.

One small positive thought can change your whole day.

ZIG ZIGLAR

Start each day with a positive affirmation. Repeat your chosen phrase out loud or in your head. It could be anything from "I am strong" to "I am good at my job". You decide what you need to work on. As you focus on your affirmation, it will soon become the truth.

Taking a warm bath has been proven to help lift your mood and steady your emotions. You don't need any fancy oils or bubbles, but there's no harm in adding some if you have them for a bit of extra luxury.

••• •••

Laugh when things don't go to plan. Maybe you spilled your coffee or missed the bus. These things can be frustrating, but if you learn to laugh when things go wrong, it will make it easier to move on from them. Harbouring anger or upset will only make you miserable.

••• •••

Practise ten minutes of yoga daily. There are plenty of free videos online so make it part of your daily routine. Calmly breathing, stretching and moving will help you feel ready to tackle any obstacles in your day.

Dream as if you'll live forever,
live as if you'll die today.

JAMES DEAN

Clear your clutter. A tidy room can help you organize your mind. You might even find some long-lost hidden treasures that you'd forgotten about. Sort your finds into piles ready to keep, throw out or give away.

Believe you can and you're halfway there.

THEODORE ROOSEVELT

Turn a bad experience into a lesson instead of a failure. When things go wrong, you can often reframe them. Maybe you burned your dinner. Don't worry. Look at it as an opportunity to learn and grow from your mistakes. There's always another option for you. Perhaps you can try the recipe again — or use it as an excuse to treat yourself to a takeout!

Start your morning with a big refreshing drink of water. Add ice or a slice of lemon if you fancy and stay hydrated throughout the day.

● ● ● (22) ● ● ●

Take a break. Get up from your desk and walk round the block or do five jumping jacks. If you spend a lot of your day standing up, make a cup of tea and sit down for five minutes.

● ● ● (23) ● ● ●

Tell someone you love them. Drop them a text, email or old-fashioned postcard. The feel-good factor will soon come bounding back to you.

Try a new recipe. The act of cooking something new and sitting down to a tasty dish will make you feel positive and nurtured. If you're not confident in the kitchen, think about ordering a recipe box where the ingredients are sent directly to you.

Just don't give up trying to do what you really want to do. Where there is love and inspiration, I don't think you can go wrong.

ELLA FITZGERALD

Find cheerleaders in your life to pick you up when you are down. This doesn't mean spending time with people who only agree with you but choosing to be with those who lift you up when you're feeling low. They will be able to point out all your good qualities, find the positive in a bad situation or simply just be with you.

Pay it forward by buying a stranger a cup of coffee. Add it to your bill and ask the serving staff to treat the next person in line. A little act of kindness can help to spread positivity.

If I cannot do great things, I can do small things in a great way.

MARTIN LUTHER KING JR

Re-read your favourite book. It will bring back all those feelings of why you loved it in the first place and you'll probably notice some new things, too. This can really help you reset and feel more positive.

Start a self-love list. Write down all the good things about yourself. Include anything from making a great cup of tea to being a kind, loyal friend. Keep it somewhere safe and refer to it whenever you're feeling the need for a boost.

There's nothing more nurturing than a steaming bowl of home-cooked soup. Raid your fridge and use up those leftover vegetables. Chopping can be very therapeutic, and you don't need to worry too much about a recipe. It will feel like warm hug in a bowl.

february

Soak up some happy beams. Lack of sunlight during the dreary winter months can really affect your mood and energy levels, so go outside for a daily fix. If you can't seem to get enough, try a vitamin D supplement or a lightbox to boost your exposure.

Why not widen your horizons with an online class? Whether you want to start crocheting, take a stand-up comedy course or learn how to decorate cakes, it's likely you'll find one online that can help you on your way. Learning something new will help you feel more positive about other aspects of your life and might even take you in a new direction.

• • • (03) • • •

Remember that the dark days of winter will pass, the sunlight will grow stronger and you will feel better again. Just hang on in there!

Grab a stack of your favourite magazines or log onto Pinterest and create a mood board to make a visual plan of your goals and dreams. You might choose pictures of a golden beach in order to keep you saving for your dream holiday, or maybe you'd love to change your career. Try printing it out and displaying it somewhere prominent to keep yourself focused and uplifted.

There's no such thing as bad weather, just the wrong clothes. Forget about the elements, wrap up warm, put on some boots and get outside. Even if you just go out for ten minutes, you'll feel better. Stomp through puddles, walk in mud and enjoy a lovely warm cuppa when you get back in.

Say STOP when you feel negative thoughts building. If you're alone, shout it out loud, but even saying the word in your mind will help, too. If you need to, imagine a big red stop sign with the word spelled out in capital letters. Pressing pause on negative thoughts for a few moments can often be all you need to reset.

Imagine yourself in five or ten years. Will the problems troubling you today matter, or will they have dissolved into nothing? Hopefully you'll find that by looking at the bigger picture, your worries will not feel so big and overwhelming.

Give the gift of your time by volunteering. Not only does it help others, but it will also lift your own spirits. There are plenty of ways you can get involved. Perhaps you can sign up to a helpline, organize charity donations or help staff a foodbank.

Create a yummy raw veg snack board with vibrantly coloured carrots and peppers to brighten up your day. Crunching on raw vegetables can release any hidden tension in your jaw and reduce feelings of stress.

A problem is a chance for you to do your best.

DUKE ELLINGTON

Go green to boost your magnesium levels and give yourself a lift. Start with one portion of spinach or another leafy green vegetable today and build from there. If you're not keen on greens, try popping a handful of spinach into your morning fruit smoothie.

Mediation is a great way to reduce stress, and best of all, you can do it anywhere. Find a quiet space where you can sit comfortably. Focus on breathing in peace and releasing any tension with your outbreath. Allow your thoughts to wander and then bring them back to focus on your breathing. Mark the end of your mediation by breathing in deeply three times. Note your positive feelings and try to revisit them throughout your day or whenever you need a boost.

Take a break from your phone. For one hour, turn it off or put it in another room. The constant notifications and interruptions can have a negative effect on your mood, so discover how it feels to be free of your phone for a short time.

It can be hard to see your own positives so ask your friends to list three things they like or admire about you. Write them down and keep them safe for the next time you're awash with self-doubt.

••• 15 •••

Do one thing that makes you happy. Maybe that's choosing the film you'd like to watch, the meal you want to eat, or where you should go for a walk. It doesn't matter how small it is; putting yourself first will remind you and others that you're important too.

••• •••

Did you know that getting enough omega-3s in your diet can help to soothe stress and boost a positive mindset? You can take supplements, but the best way to get these nutrients is to eat two or three portions of oily fish a week.

••• (17) •••

Sing! Join a choir, download a karaoke app or belt out a song in the shower. Singing has been proven to boost the mood and will help you feel happier even when the tunes are no longer playing.

••• (18) •••

Head out into nature with no distractions. Don't take your phone or listen to music; instead, look around you and notice the natural wonder all around.

Spring clean your sleep routine for a good night's rest and a more positive outlook. Stay off your screen for an hour before bed and keep your bedroom clutter free. Try to avoid working in the same place that you sleep in order to associate your room with calm and rest.

●●● 20 ●●●

Breakfast really is the most important meal, so make it a celebration to start your day. Take the time to sit at the table and really enjoy your food. Create a vibrant plate with plenty of fresh fruit and play your favourite music. Savour your food and give yourself everything you need to start your day right.

21

Choosing to be positive and having a grateful attitude will determine how you're going to live your life.

JOEL OSTEEN

It's all too easy to feel overwhelmed at work, so make sure you reach out and ask for help if you need it. Often the support of a colleague is just what you need to help you feel more positive about a tricky task, so try inviting someone from your office for coffee in order to brainstorm your project or get advice.

Why not mix yourself a mocktail mid-week to avoid a work-day hangover? You don't have to forgo alcohol completely but a few alcohol-free days a week will help you avoid those post-drinking blues the day after. Best of all, you'll have a clearer head and will sleep better, too.

Listen to your internal voice. No, not the one saying the negative things, but the one that reminds you of your hope and dreams. Did you always want to write a book or travel? Examine how you can make these come true.

Put some change in a savings jar. It could be a coin or two, or a note — whatever you have. Add the same amount each day and by the end of the year you'll have a substantial amount to treat yourself to something you couldn't afford before.

•••(26)•••

Tackle your to-do list with positivity and purpose. Why not write your chores in brightly coloured pens on a white board or piece of paper and then tick them off as you go? It will be hard to feel gloomy if you've got a rainbow of jobs to complete.

•••(27)•••

Pick your favourite sport and join a team. You don't need to be any good; simply playing a competitive game with others will boost your mood. You'll have fun and keep fit, too!

Take a spontaneous trip. Jump on a train or bus and head to an unknown destination. Make sure you pack enough water and snacks and be sure you can get back safely, but other than that, don't over think it. Just enjoy the adventure.

Cuddle a hot water bottle or microwavable bean bag and enjoy the heat sensation spreading through your body. It's not quite as good as a hug with a real person but the warmth and the five minutes of calm will help you reset.

march

End your day with an evaluation. How did it go today? Did you achieve everything you needed to? Was there anything you could have done better? What did you do well? Celebrate your achievements and write some goals to carry that positivity into tomorrow.

Staring at a screen all day can drain your positive energy as well as dry your eyes. Why not try taking regular screen breaks if you're spending a lot of time looking at a screen. Adopt the 20-20-20 trick where you focus on something 20 feet (6 metres) in the distance, for 20 seconds every 20 minutes.

Clear your garden or help out in a community space. Now is the perfect time to cut back plants, prune roses and gather the dead wood that has accumulated over winter. By spending time outside and preparing for spring, you'll find your own mind is drawn to new beginnings.

••• **04** •••

Watch your language and try to only use positive words and descriptions. It will soon become part of your natural thought process to see and say the good things in life.

••• (05) •••

Set your alarm early to take advantage of the fact the days are slowly growing longer. Make a hot drink and pause to appreciate the rising sun.

••• (06) •••

Whether you live alone or share your space, create some house rules so everyone feels happy with their day-to-day living. These could include a practical cleaning schedule or a rota for who buys the milk. Write them out and pin them up for everyone to see. The team spirit will keep everyone feeling positive and motivated.

••• (07) •••

Brighten up your day with some flowers. If you can't afford to buy a bunch, find some wild flowers or simply go for a walk to look at the blossom on the trees.

We all need to blow off steam sometimes so why not find a private place, grab a pillow and scream into it? Even better, have a good old shout out loud. It's a great way to feel more positive and ready to tackle any problems with a slightly clearer head.

A champion is defined not by their wins but by how they can recover when they fall.

SERENA WILLIAMS

••• 10 •••

Take 10 minutes to go "plogging", the Swedish concept of jogging and litter picking. Run around your local area picking up any rogue cans or bits of paper. You'll get some fresh air, fitness and satisfaction.

Check up on a neighbour. There's so much positivity to found in creating a close community in the area where you live. Not only will you feel great, but they'll appreciate knowing there's a helping hand just a few doors away.

12

You're braver than you believe, and stronger than you seem, and smarter than you think.

A. A. MILNE

●●● (13) ●●●

Book yourself in for a massage. Even just 15 minutes can boost your levels of oxytocin to keep the feel-good factor in your system for up to 48 hours.

●●● (14) ●●●

Open a window and breathe in the fresh air for five or ten breaths. Better still, step outside. It might be cold, but that will help you feel more alert and invigorated, ready to tackle your next task.

●●● (15) ●●●

Give yourself permission to be you. You may find life starts to get easier when you are your more authentic self.

···● 16 ●···

It isn't always easy, but saying sorry can help to clear the air, maintain good relationships with the people around you and take a weight off your shoulders. Holding a grudge can be the road to negative thinking, so instead find the person you've disagreed with and make a genuine apology.

···● 17 ●···

A positive person is someone who always looks for the opportunities in events that come their way, big or small. And it is never too late to live a life without regrets. Best of all you can decide to start today. It could be as simple as accepting an invitation for a coffee.

Create a positive routine, whether that means finding time for exercise, cooking a healthy meal at the end of the day or making a date to see your best friend. It's good to stick to the things that make you feel happy in the long term.

If you don't like the road you're walking, start paving another one.

DOLLY PARTON

······

Sometimes it can feel as if your problems are weighing you down. But instead of worrying, choose one problem each day to examine. Try asking yourself if there's anything you can do to change it. If not, then move on. Only deal with the problems you can control; anything else is a waste of energy.

···● (21) ●···

Make your home a positive place to be. This could mean loading the dishwasher before you leave for work or creating a cosy reading corner. It will really help you feel uplifted if you're returning to a calming environment.

Have a secret phrase that you can repeat silently when the going gets tough. You don't need to tell anyone what it is, but have it ready to deal with any negative situations at home or work.

••• (23) •••

Treat yourself to some you time, whether it's by getting a coffee or sitting down for ten minutes with a book or your favourite TV show. Remember there's always time to look after your well-being.

••• (24) •••

Comparison really is the thief of joy. Just be happy being you. If everyone was the same, life would be rather boring.

Act as if what you do makes
a difference. It does.

WILLIAM JAMES

Lie on your back and watch the clouds drift by.
Perhaps you can see the shapes of faces or animals
in them, or maybe you can notice their different
textures against the sky. Just a few minutes' cloud-
gazing can remind you of how life moves on and
all things eventually change.

●●● (27) ●●●

Visit your favourite woodland or forest and hug a tree. Wrapping your arms around a sturdy trunk and feeling the rough bark against your cheek will help you feel grounded. Yes, you might feel a bit silly at first, but that's all part of the fun!

●●● (28) ●●●

Sign up to a positive news website. It will deliver uplifting stories to boost your mood, however flat you're feeling.

●●● (29) ●●●

Remember a time you felt passionate about something. What was it? How did it feel? Think about how you can recreate that feeling with something new.

If you truly pour your heart into what you believe in, even if it makes you vulnerable, amazing things can and will happen.

EMMA WATSON

••• 31 •••

Why save everything for a special occasion when you can make today that day? Wear your favourite outfit, drink the expensive wine and use the fancy plates. After all, every day is special, right?

april

01

Do one thing to be the change you're hoping to see in your life. If you'd like your friends to call you more, why not call them? Or if you'd like someone to bring you breakfast in bed or buy you flowers for no reason, why not do that for someone?

02

Volunteer for something instead of waiting to be given a job. It could be heading up a project at work or a big chore that needs to be done at home. Not only will you feel more in control, but you'll also get a big sense of satisfaction when it's complete.

03

Above all, be the heroine of your life, not the victim.

NORA EPHRON

Take some time to daydream. It may seem like a waste of time, but it will allow your creativity to flow.

•••(05)•••

Remember that no one owes you anything in your life. It's up to you to make things happen. You'll soon realize it means the possibilities are limitless.

Make a fun movie on your phone with friends. Get together to write a rough script and get your costumes together. It might not be Hollywood standard, but you'll probably have a lot more fun.

••• 07 •••

It's so easy to rush around trying to get lots of things done, but why not try focusing on just one thing? This way you will get the task done more efficiently and by throwing yourself one hundred per cent into something, you might also enjoy it a bit more.

Do one thing every day
that scares you.

ELEANOR ROOSEVELT

Fake it until you make it! Even if you're not feeling your most confident, act as though you are and soon it will be the truth. Just try it.

● ● ● 10 ● ● ●

There's really no need to say unkind things about other people. If you do find yourself starting to say something negative about someone, try to counterbalance it with something positive. It will make you feel better to see the good in people, too. After all, no one is perfect.

Look at your life through a lens of positivity. Instead of telling yourself you have to go to the gym, try saying "I get to go to the gym". When you start to see things as a privilege rather than a chore, even the dullest job will seem like a joy.

Eat a meal in a different place in your home. For instance, if you always eat breakfast in the kitchen, try sitting on the sofa or going outside to shake up your routine.

•••(13)•••

Go camping. If you don't have a tent, borrow one or find a campsite that has tents already put up. Pack lots of warm clothes and some marshmallows to toast. Then all you need to do is light a fire and gaze at the stars.

14

Wherever you go, no matter what the weather, always bring your own sunshine.

ANTHONY J. D'ANGELO

Spending time in nature boosts your mood, so why not try a mindful nature-based activity such as whittling? Grab a vegetable peeler or small knife and head to your local woods to find the perfect stick. Carve away from yourself as you strip off the bark.

Cook up a big batch of your favourite food. Put on some music and enjoy the process. By making extra portions for the week ahead, you'll be doing your future self a favour, too!

Hold a pub quiz for friends. Either invite them round to your house or meet in an actual pub. Remember not to make the questions too hard so everyone can get a few answers right.

•••(18)•••

Dream big... and then make a plan. This will keep you moving toward your goal before you get disheartened. It's easier to take small steps than one big leap.

Why not treat yourself to the simple joy of stone-skimming. Any river, lake or sea will do. Find a large flat stone and throw it into the water. See how many times you can make it skip over the surface.

Surprise a friend with a delivery of home-baked goods, a homemade card or simply a doorstep visit. You'll both feel invigorated to spend some unplanned, unpressured time together.

Take time to focus on everything your body can do, instead of the things it can't. For example, your smile can cheer up a stranger and your brain can recreate happy memories.

Choose experiences over possessions. It might mean that instead of buying that new pair of shoes today, you put the money aside toward a short city break or week away in the future, which will impact your life more deeply.

••• 23 •••

When it rains, resist the urge to hide indoors. Instead jump in a puddle and reconnect with your inner child.

Create an end of work ritual. Maybe it's changing your clothes, a short walk outside or a cup of tea. It will help you make a healthy transition between work and rest.

Laugh out loud. It won't be long until the real chuckles start to come and the feel-good endorphins flood your body.

••••(26)••••

The best time to plant a tree was 20 years ago. The second best time is now.

PROVERB

Head to the countryside or visit a farm and look out for some spring babies. From lambs to calves to chicks, you'll see new life springing up around you. It won't fail to lift your mood.

●●● 28 ●●●

Take some time to write a list of your values and think about how they can be reflected in your life. For example, if family time is important, then maybe a job that means long hours in the office is not for you.

Hit the play park. Go on the swings, whizz down the zip wire and spin on the roundabout. Acting like a little kid will help free you of the burdens you're carrying with you, at least for a little while.

•••(30)•••

Take a probiotic or try to eat more gut-friendly foods such as live yoghurt and oats. A happy gut often equals a happy mind.

may

There is often nothing nicer than wading into cold water with your bare feet. Try dipping your toes into a river or paddling in the sea for a quick positivity boost.

Spend some quality time with a pet. Even if you can't have a pet of your own, see if you can borrow one for a bit. Walking a dog, stroking a cat or even chatting to a budgie can all help to soothe anxiety and take your mind off your worries.

••• 03 •••

Climb a mountain (or a large hill). You will feel on top of the world and you'll get to experience amazing views. It will be breathtaking and rewarding, reminding you that putting in the effort is always worth it.

••• 04 •••

Treat yourself to an afternoon tea. Make or buy your favourite cake, use a cute mug or tea cup and lay the table nicely. Pop some flowers in a vase and then sit down to a decadent mid-afternoon meal.

••• (05) •••

Create a treasure hunt for family or friends. Inside or outside doesn't matter; simply create the clues and remember to provide a prize.

••• (06) •••

Teach others what you know. Whether it's a work colleague or a friend you're coaching, you'll help someone else reach their potential and also cement your own skills.

••• (07) •••

Share your worries. If you don't have a good friend for family member you can talk to, consider meeting with a life coach or therapist. They will help you see things more clearly and show you a way to move forward.

Go to a penny arcade. It won't cost the earth and you'll soon find yourself engrossed in trying to win extra coins. You'll get a big boost if you hit the jackpot.

Keep your regular wake-up time the same, or at least within the same hour or two. Experts have found that people who stick to regular sleeping and waking time will have a better mood and feel more able to cope with the obstacles life places in their path.

10

Whatever you are, be a good one.

WILLIAM MAKEPEACE THACKERY

Cover your home in positive post-it notes. Copy some quotes from this book or some other personal affirmations and put them all over your bedroom, bathroom and kitchen.

••• (12) •••

Try chewing gum for around five minutes. Research shows that this rhythmic action will release serotonin and boost your mood.

Free yourself from the idea that you have to be perfect. Your very best really is the very best.

Love your body and mind by treating it to healthy, wholesome food. It can sometimes feel like a treat to dive into a tub of ice cream — and we're certainly not going to stop you. Treat yourself to some TLC in the form of a fresh fruit smoothie some days, too. By keeping your body nourished with fresh fruit and veg, you'll find your mind gets a boost.

••• (15) •••

Allow yourself to get bored. Research shows that by not filling your time with activities and chores, a period of boredom will allow your brain to relax and reboot.

••• (16) •••

Create a memory box of all your happy times. Include anything from photos, notes or mementoes and whenever you need a boost, just peek inside.

••• (17) •••

Save your favourite treats for the most special occasions. Make sure you really value whatever you're treating yourself to and keep your rewards fresh to avoid them becoming boring.

●●● ●●●

If you ever find yourself feeling low after scrolling through your phone, it might be time for a spring clean. Replace any apps bringing you down with positive ones, such as good news notifications or inspirational quotes.

●●● ●●●

Some days there won't be a song in your heart. Sing anyway.

EMORY AUSTIN

Give your wardrobe a makeover. Take out all your clothes and try them on. Get rid of anything that doesn't fit or that you haven't worn in ages or that doesn't make you feel great.

Look up funny videos on the internet and give yourself five minutes to really chuckle. Watching dogs wearing sunglasses or kids doing silly things is bound to raise your spirits.

••• 22 •••

Take a moment to reminisce and think about how far you've come. Time to give yourself a big congratulations!

●●● 23 ●●●

Great sleep will help you feel great. Try a few drops of lavender oil on your pillow before you drift off — it will help you fall more quickly into a gentle slumber.

24

Fearlessness is like a muscle... the more I exercise it the more natural it becomes to not let my fears run me.

ARIANNA HUFFINGTON

Set an intention for your day. This could be promising yourself you will stay calm for a meeting or you will smile at a stranger. This way you'll find you start each day with a positive focus which will hopefully trickle down into all areas of your life.

Life goes by fast. Enjoy it. Calm down. It's all funny.

JOAN RIVERS

When you have a negative thought, challenge it. Ask yourself what makes it true. More often than not, it's just something you've created in your mind.

••• 28 •••

Slouching can make life seem harder and gloomier. If you notice yourself slumping, try an exaggerated shrug. Lift your shoulders up to your ears and then drop them downward with a big breath out. Repeat a few times.

••• 29 •••

Plan a weekend away, either with friends or on your own. Choose somewhere you feel relaxed and you won't have to fulfil any responsibilities. Just focus on having fun.

**Always keep your eyes open.
Keep watching. Because whatever
you see can inspire you.**

GRACE CODDINGTON

Settle on the sofa with some popcorn and watch
your favourite rom-com. Switching off from real
life and inhabiting your fantasy will help you feel
happier in an instant.

june

Try upcycling a piece of furniture. Choose something you already own or pick an item up from a thrift store. All you need is some paint and your imagination. You've got nothing to lose and you'll get a massive boost when you complete your unique creation.

Take a rainbow walk. Head outside and try to gather items that represent each colour of the rainbow. Red leaves, orange petals and so on. When you get home display them on a windowsill for an uplifting dash of colour.

••• (03) •••

Make a feel-good playlist packed full of your favourite calming or uplifting songs.

••• (04) •••

If you feel like you need to hide away from the world for a bit, then make a den. Get a cozy blanket, cushions and nest away in a corner of your room. Take a good book and some snacks, too.

If you get tired, learn to rest, not quit.

BANKSY

Research has shown that jolts and bumps can actually improve our mood. So, take your bike off-road and try bumping down a muddy track for a mood-boost. Or run down a steep hill fast to create the same effect.

By looking after your body, you're also looking after your mind. If you work at a desk, take time to ensure your workstation is comfortable and safe, with your computer screen properly aligned and your chair at the right level. If you drive a car or operate machinery, check the positioning so everything is safe and comfortable.

• • • 08 • • •

Play some air guitar. You might feel silly at first, but when you get into it you might not be able to stop!

• • • 09 • • •

Go and see a comedy show or spend time with a funny friend. It's hard to worry about your problems when you're busy laughing!

Next time you're out for a walk, transform it into a mini adventure. Take some dice with you and let them guide your way. When you reach a crossroads, roll the dice and go left on an even number or right on an odd. Keep this up every time you need to make a choice.

Create a happy shelf or box where you keep your favourite photos and mementoes. Be sure to visit it whenever you're feeling down.

Rolling down a hill is something children love to do and there's a reason for that. It's because it makes you feel good. Just try it and see.

●●●● 13 ●●●

Get yourself a house plant or two. Caring for something and keeping it alive will give you a challenge and a sense of satisfaction. Some plants also purify the air.

●●●● 14 ●●●

Shout your worries into a worry jar. Any old vase or jam jar will do — just say what's on your mind and then tip it away. It might feel silly, but it's a great way to start feeling better.

15

Done is better than perfect.

SHERYL SANDBERG

De-stress by turning your thumbs horizontally and placing them just beneath your eyebrows on the bridge of your nose. Press firmly for ten seconds while breathing slowly. Now move them to the outside of your eyebrows with your index finger slightly above, press again and continue to breathe for another ten seconds.

Take a nap if you're feeling drained; but don't just drift off in a chair, do it properly. Set your alarm, shut your curtains and lie down. Limit it to 30 minutes, otherwise you could wake up feeling groggy.

Make a list of odd jobs around your home and set your mind to some DIY. There are plenty of videos on YouTube if you need some advice. You'll feel a great sense of satisfaction when you tick off those tasks.

Sign up for a race — whether it's running, biking, swimming or an obstacle course. It doesn't matter how well you do, having a goal will motivate you to train regularly. And you might surprise yourself with your performance.

Take some time out in nature and go foraging. Try picking up some driftwood for an art project, or even gather some nettles to make a delicious soup.

••• 21 •••

Cut down on sugar, caffeine and additives. Focus on eating wholefoods, herbal teas and healthy foods for a month. It shouldn't take too long to feel a physical and mental boost.

While out walking gather some large flat stones to build a stone tower. This meditative exercise will leave you feeling balanced and uplifted. Just be sure to put all your stones back to where you found them.

Ask an older member of your family or friend to teach you a skill such as knitting or baking a cake. Not only will you learn something, but they'll feel valued and appreciated, too. It's also a great way to spend quality time together.

•••(24)•••

Give someone a surprise gift. It doesn't have to be expensive, just something that says you were thinking of them.

••• (25) •••

Learning a new language has many benefits. It
has been proven to improve memory function,
enhance creative thinking capacity and make you
feel good. You can pick up free courses online or
attend a class and increase your social circle, too.

••• (26) •••

Once you choose hope, anything's possible.

CHRISTOPHER REEVE

Whether you want something fun or you're looking for a challenge, try doing a jigsaw. It will help you slow down and will feel quite calming, while giving you a boost once completed.

Be a tourist in your home town and check onto a guided tour. You might think you know your area pretty well, but an organized tour will reveal different parts of a city to you. Often there are themes such as ghost walks, local legends and so on. You'll start to see your neighbourhood differently.

29

No matter what people tell you, words and ideas can change the world.

ROBIN WILLIAMS

Soothe away stresses by practising self-massage either on your head, hands or feet. Use some calming oils or lotions and take some time to loosen any knots any relieve tension.

july

Take advantage of the warmer weather and practise *shinrin-yoku*, the Japanese art of forest bathing. Walk into the woods and focus on the how the leaves move on the trees and the patterns made by the sunlight shining through. Tune in to bird calls and notice the fresh smells and sounds. Choose to walk slowly or find a place to sit as you take it all in.

Find a small foot bridge over a flowing river and play "Pooh sticks" with a friend. Drop your sticks over one side of the bridge then race to the other side to see which who wins.

Eat your evening meal earlier. Not only will it help you digest your food, but it will also prevent you from overeating and improve the quality of your sleep, all of which will help you boost your well-being.

If you look at what you have in life, you'll always have more.

OPRAH WINFREY

•••(05)•••

Take the TV and any other devices that have blinking red lights out of your room. They may seem small, but they can really wreck your sleep. If that's not possible, consider wearing an eye mask in bed. You'll be amazed how positive you feel in the morning after a quality snooze.

Treat yourself to an uplifting shower by using a fragrant body wash. Mint or grapefruit are two of the best smells for getting you in the mood to have a good day.

••• (07) •••

Go for a walk and gather some stones. Arrange them in a spiral, starting with the largest at the centre and building outward. Notice how the spiral is never-ending and never completed. Like the stone spiral, you can keep growing and expanding to your own design.

••• (08) •••

Have a good old cry. Crying releases feel-good hormones, which make you feel better almost immediately.

··••··

Go birdwatching. Even if you haven't got fancy binoculars, you'll still be able to study some feathered friends.

··••··

Always take the opportunity to speak up, even if it means disagreeing with someone. They may not agree with you, but they will respect you. And you'll feel more at ease because you were true to yourself.

··•(11)•··

Write an email or letter to someone you care about telling them all your favourite things about them. It will give you both a big positivity boost.

12

You are enough just as you are.

MEGHAN MARKLE

Host an international evening. Ask friends or family to dress up and bring a dish from another country. Maybe they could find out some interesting facts about their chosen country, too. Delicious food and learning about different cultures are always a good mix.

The purpose of life is to discover your gift... The meaning of life is to give your gift away.

DAVID VISCOTT

Commit to trying something new. It could be a new food, walking route or skill. Whatever it is, step out of your comfort zone — you could surprise yourself.

•••(16)•••

Hang in a hammock. If you don't have one, try to borrow or make one. Outside is best and the gentle sway will help you unwind and relax your mind.

Stretching isn't just for cats. Set aside five minutes each day to stretch out your body. Not only will you feel more relaxed, but it will prevent injury and back pain, too.

Next time you're out on a walk, take a piece of paper and pencil to try shadow tracing. Put your paper underneath a branch or leaf and trace the outline of the shadow. Focus on the small details to really enjoy the experience.

19

Pick one thing to forgive yourself for, write it on a piece of paper and then rip it up or burn it (safely!).

20

Being positive is a sign of intelligence.

MAXIME LAGACÉ

21

Gather some friends and try an escape room activity. You'll have to work together as a team to solve clues within a certain time. You'll feel more energized to tackle other tricky tasks, too.

●●● (22) ●●●

Start your day with a power hour — an extra hour you can create by waking up earlier. It will mean setting your alarm, but it will be worth it. You could exercise, write in a journal or get some life admin done.

●●● (23) ●●●

Sort through your wardrobe and find a pile of clothes you've been intending to mend. Maybe it's sewing on a button or fixing a hole. Spend the afternoon stitching and you'll soon have a whole new outfit to wear.

Schedule some free time into your calendar. It's crucial to take the time you need for yourself, even if it's just 30 minutes a day. You'll get back to your tasks feeling recharged and accomplish a lot more than if you worked straight through.

Take a different route home from work or to the shops. It will make your routine feel fresh and get your brain working rather than running on autopilot.

Positivity always wins... Always.

GARY VAYNERCHUK

••• •••

Add a green break to your day. Even if you're in an urban setting, find a park or body of water to visit on your lunch break or when you finish work. Just take a few moments to breathe in your environment and take in the sights.

••• (28) •••

Print out a selection of photos from your phone and get them framed or make a collage. Put them somewhere you can see them every day to bring a smile to your face.

29

Head to a natural area and see if you can track an animal. Look for droppings or footprints. Even if you don't find what you're tracking, you'll have been on an exciting adventure.

30

By being yourself, you put something wonderful in the world that was not there before.

EDWIN ELLIOT

31

Make some land art using sticks, stones and leaves. Your creativity may surprise you.

august

Grab a colouring book and some coloured pencils or pens and get shading. It will soothe your mind and release any pent-up tension.

Decorate some stones with positive slogans or smiling faces and leave them around your local area for others to find. You could even add a hashtag to share photos of the stones on social media.

Building a sandcastle isn't just for kids. There's something deeply satisfying when you fill a bucket with damp sand and tip it out to form a mound. Maybe you'll find yourself building an entire village!

Teach yourself origami, the Japanese art of paper folding. All you need is some paper and online instructions or a book and soon you'll be creating the most wonderful paper animals and flowers. The calming process will boost your positivity.

Treat yourself to an ice-cream or lolly. Settle down somewhere quiet to watch the world go by as you savour the ice-cold treat.

●●● **06** ●●●

Make a daisy chain by gathering together some long-stalked daisies. Carefully make a slit in each stem and thread the next daisy through before repeating. Wear it as a necklace or crown or gift to a friend.

●●● **07** ●●●

Go mudlarking. Treasures are often hidden in muddy riverbanks and estuaries, especially if you visit at low tide. Take a bucket and spade and borrow a metal detector if you can. Just make sure you're safe, and wear some waterproof shoes!

••• (08) •••

It always seems impossible until it is done.

NELSON MANDELA

••• (09) •••

Head to the beach and do some beachcombing. You'll find all sorts of shells, driftwood and washed-up treasures. Use them to create an art installation with the beach as a natural canvas.

••• (10) •••

Climbing trees is a lost art. The act of clambering up some branches will release any tension and help you feel like a kid again.

Next time you're waiting for a bus or in a queue at the shops, strike up a conversation with a senior citizen. Older people are sometimes lonely, and they usually have the great stories to tell. They could even give you helpful advice for problems you may be facing.

Plant a seed. Fill a pot with earth, make a hole and bury your seed. Water it and put it somewhere warm with natural light. You'll have plenty to look forward to as you wait for the shoots to peep through.

Start a nature diary, jotting down or sketching anything new you see around you. You could add a few things every day or week and track how your local environment changes over time. Feeling connected to nature is a powerful boost to positivity.

Eat a square of dark chocolate. It's been proven to lift the mood and improve health.

•••(15)•••

Challenge your friends and family to dress up as their favourite characters or celebrities. There will be some great outfits that are bound to leave you laughing and with great positive memories.

16

Find a spot in a park or café and watch the world go by. It will make you feel more connected and uplifted.

17

Inspiration comes from within yourself. One has to be positive. When you're positive, good things happen.

DEEP ROY

18

Go fly a kite — just as Mary Poppins suggests! You can even make one if you're feeling creative.

Spied a new café on your way to work? A new restaurant opened up in your neighbourhood? Plan a visit and check it out. Take a friend and experience it together. Trying new things will help you feel more positive and you'll be supporting a new business.

Go through your social media accounts and unfollow anyone whose posts make you feel unhappy. Instead, follow accounts that post things that bring you joy — whether that's funny cat memes, gorgeous travel photos or hunks with hummus (yes, it's a thing!).

••• 21 •••

A spoonful of honey can help reduce inflammation in the brain, which can help to improve low moods.

Join a club. It could be chess, singing or gardening. Whatever it is, make a commitment to try something new and meet different people. By challenging yourself, you'll see just how much you're capable of and feel more positive about all aspects of life.

Whenever you're online shopping, tick the gift option and then write yourself a little note, such as "you're going to look great in this" or "you deserve this". Then when your parcel does arrive, you'll have a little boost as well as new swag.

••• 24 •••

Whatever you do, do it well.

WALT DISNEY

••• 25 •••

Hold a yard sale outside your house. While it's a great way to get rid of clutter, you'll meet your neighbours and raise some money, too.

••• 26 •••

Paint your garden fence or a wall of your home a different colour. Whether it's baby pink or bright green, grab a paint brush and some paint and get going. You'll feel a sense of achievement and have brightened the place up.

27

If you know a frazzled new parent, offer to take care of the baby while they have a nap or uninterrupted shower. It could make their day — and you'll feel pretty good for having helped, too.

28

Nothing is impossible. The word itself says "I'm possible!"

AUDREY HEPBURN

29

Do something that you've always wanted to try. Whether it's hiking up a mountain or attending a life-drawing art class, feel the fear and do it anyway.

• • • (30) • • •

Bake some bread. The process of measuring the ingredients and kneading the dough will have a calming effect on your mind, allowing your thoughts to flow. And there's something inherently uplifting about the smell of fresh bread wafting through your home!

Take your family or friends on a scavenger hunt. Write a list of things they need to find and they can either collect them or take a photo. Don't be limited to nature — an urban hunt is just as much fun.

september

Pick a favourite tree and pay it a visit. Make notes about its appearance or even sketch it out. You can come back and repeat this throughout the year. Watch as green leaves may turn yellow or squirrels start to visit as they gather nuts for winter. The connection with a single point in nature will help you feel connected and boost your positivity.

If someone loses their temper with you, maybe at work or in the supermarket queue, remember that you while you can't control other people's actions, you can control your reactions. Try to stay and think about if they're coming from a place of fear or anxiety. You'll feel better in the long term.

Don't judge each day by the harvest you reap but by the seeds that you plant.

ROBERT LOUIS STEVENSON

•••(04)•••

Sign up to be a mentor either at work or another organization. When you start to help someone less experienced than you, you'll see how much you are capable of.

•••(05)•••

Set up a free library outside your home. Build or buy a waterproof box, fill it with books and write a sign inviting passers-by to take or leave a book. You could even include a notepad and pen to encourage messages and reviews.

Squash your negative thoughts with positive ones. Each time you think something bad about yourself, think of two good things. Soon it will become a habit to muffle your negative thinking and replace it with positivity.

Sometimes all you need is a holiday to feel more positive. If you can't take a real one, try taking one in your mind for a few minutes. Picture yourself sitting on a beach, listening to the waves, smelling the ocean and feeling the warm sand beneath your feet. Close your eyes and really focus on the smells and sounds of your imaginary trip.

Splash out on some new stationery for that good old back-to-school feeling. A blank page is begging to be filled with great ideas.

Positive anything is better than negative nothing.

ELBERT HUBBARD

Find someone you can give a huge cuddle to. Hugs will help boost your well-being and spread positivity to the person you're hugging.

Get grounded by taking off your shoes and socks and walking outside. Sink your feet into the grass, sand, water or mud. Spread your toes and feel your weight reaching downward toward your feet. Close your eyes and take several deep breaths.

When you're stuck in a negative thought, try tapping your fingers rhythmically for a few minutes. This can help reset your brain and boost your feel-good hormones.

●●● (13) ●●●

Try drinking a cup of hot water and lemon. It will cleanse your system of tension-causing toxins, and the vitamin C in the lemon can help to enhance your mood.

••• •••

Get a change of scene. If you live in the country, head to the city or the coast. Just having a different view to look out on or getting away from your everyday situation can help make your mental outlook more positive.

••• •••

Think big thoughts but relish small pleasures.

H. JACKSON BROWN JR

Remember to plant bulbs for spring. Put a selection in your garden, in plant pots or even in a public space and forget about them. Then when spring comes you'll be treated to a colourful, uplifting flower show.

●●● (17) ●●●

Send a copy of your favourite book to a friend. Sharing is a great way to boost positivity on both sides!

●●● (18) ●●●

Pull on your shoes and go for a jog or brisk walk. Research has shown that five minutes of green exercise – activity in the presence of nature – offers a greater boost to mood and self-esteem than longer periods inside.

Ask yourself what one small thing you can do to make your day more fun. It could be chatting with a friend or taking a dance class.

I'm thankful for my struggle because without it I wouldn't have stumbled across my strength.

ALEX ELLE

Try cold water swimming. Research shows that it activates endorphins and gives you a natural high.

Take a day trip to a beauty spot. Seeing awe-inspiring nature before you in a breathtaking vista will always do the job of boosting your positivity.

••• (23) •••

Practise mindful eating. Sit calmly and quietly and really notice what's on your plate; look at the colours and textures. As you put the food in your mouth notice how it feels and how the flavours develop as you begin to chew. Put your cutlery down between each bite to really focus on each mouthful.

Set up a ball game in your local park and invite all your friends and their families to take part. See if you can rope in some strangers, too. This way you'll be creating a sense of community and fun.

It's probably a habit you've left in your childhood, but try to make some time to doodle. This creative release may provide some answers or just help you feel calmer and more positive about your day.

••• (26) •••

Adopt a power stance by standing with your legs just wider than shoulders and your hands on your hips. Keep your chest out and chin up. Then say or think about your goal. You should feel strong and powerful.

Embrace the glorious
mess that you are.

ELIZABETH GILBERT

Make a date — with yourself. Turn down any invitations, put on your comfy clothes, grab a blanket and curl up on the sofa with your favourite book. Spending time with yourself will help you reset and gather energy.

• • • (29) • • •

Host a potluck supper where everyone brings a different dish. Try to organize people to bring savoury and sweet dishes so you don't end up with lots of the same thing. Sharing food with others creates a really positive vibe, and it helps that one person isn't stuck in the kitchen cooking all evening.

• • • (30) • • •

Put on your favourite podcast while you're doing a boring chore such as loading the dishwasher. It will turn it into a more relaxing, educational and enjoyable moment.

october

Set up a swishing party to swap clothes and replenish your wardrobe for free. Everyone brings five good quality items they no longer want, then hangs them on a rail, and everyone can choose some clothes to try on and take home.

Pack some sandwiches and a rug and head out for a picnic. It's really invigorating to go for a long walk and then simply stop in a field for your lunch whenever you feel hungry.

Give yourself a full body scan. Check to see where there are areas of tension. Simply by noticing you can start to feel better.

Send a postcard or letter — to yourself. Write a positive quote or message and pop it in the postbox. Future you will thank you!

I believe if you put out positive vibes to everybody, that's all you're going to get back.

KESHA

Change your hairstyle. It can be anything from your parting, the length or the colour. A change is a great way to reinvigorate yourself.

● ● ● (07) ● ● ●

Do a forward roll. Not only will it get the blood pumping round your body, you'll also enjoy a new sense of perspective on things.

••• •••

08

Listen to some eighties pop. The mix of upbeat tunes and nostalgia will have you feeling happy in no time.

••• **09** •••

Try eating something new. Maybe it's a fruit or vegetable you've not tasted before or a whole cuisine such as Vietnamese street food. Eating something new reminds you that the world is full of different experiences and possibilities.

••• **10** •••

Play with some artificial slime. The sensation of it oozing through your fingers will immediately relax and de-stress you.

Take a weight training class to feel the benefits of lifting heavy weights. You'll see yourself grow stronger, which will boost your self-confidence. Plus, you'll feel motivated if you're trying to reach a goal.

Treat yourself to a five-minute cake. Simply use a fork to mix four tablespoons of sugar, four of self-raising flour, two of cocoa powder and an egg in the biggest mug you have. Add three tablespoons of milk, three of vegetable oil and some vanilla essence, then pop it in the microwave on high for two minutes. Grab a spoon and enjoy!

••• •••

13

Mix things up by starting the day with a bath instead of a shower or eat breakfast for dinner — anything that helps change your view and break up your routine will give you a brain boost.

14

Sit by an open fire and allow the gentle crackling sound of the flames to wash over you. Even a BBQ or fire pit outside will help you feel relaxed and more positive.

●●●(15)●●●

Say yes, and you'll figure it out afterward.

TINA FEY

●●●(16)●●●

Spend the day doing absolutely nothing. Don't catch up on your laundry, ignore the dishes and just relax. A day resting can do wonders for your mind and body.

••• (**17**) •••

Swallow your frog. This means doing the hardest thing on your list first. You'll find that once you've cleared that hurdle, the rest of your day is plain sailing.

••• (**18**) •••

Go green and see how many ways you can protect the planet. Recycling, reusing and reducing the amount of waste you produce may seem like small things, but they can make a big difference. And knowing that you're contributing to the future of our planet will be a great boost.

••• (**19**) •••

Smile at everyone you meet today. A smile is catching, and you'll be amazed at how many beaming grins you get back. Plus, it will make you feel better inside, too.

••• 20 •••

Surround yourself with positive people. If you do have to see someone who makes you feel anything less than amazing, try to limit your time with them or see them in a group. That way you can dilute their negative impact on you.

••• 21 •••

Remember to keep thinking positively when you are facing a difficult situation. There are plenty of things you can do to smooth the way. Try to scenario plan by working out how the other person might react and then prepare your own reactions. By staying positive and focused you will be able to take the heat out of any potentially tricky situation.

Put pen to paper and start doodling to engage the creative upper right side of your brain. This will give you the space you need to allow positive thoughts to fill your mind.

Do a dot-to-dot or spot the difference puzzle. Yes, they're usually for kids, but doing something that you find easy and that will take you back to childhood is a great boost for positivity.

••• 24 •••

Create your own mini spa at home with an invigorating body scrub. Combine two cups of brown sugar with one cup of soft coconut oil. You can add your own essential oils before you apply to your skin. Scrub well and rinse off in the shower.

25

When you are enthusiastic about what you do, you feel this positive energy. It's very simple.

PAULO COELHO

Add mindfulness to your daily walk. Look around you and really notice the sights and sounds. Take a moment to stop and breathe in. What does the air feel like as it enters your nose and flows in your lungs? Focus on how you feel before and after the walk.

••• (27) •••

Reading can really lift your mood. For times when you're not able to read, instead plug in to an uplifting audiobook as a good alternative.

••• (28) •••

Pick up a yo-yo and try to learn some stunts. You'll giggle as it flies away from you but it will also boost your mood when you master a new trick.

••• (29) •••

Learn to practise self-reiki. This ancient healing will help you to connect your emotional and physical well-being by connecting with your internal energy. You'll feel more in control and positive.

Sort your inbox by taking five minutes to unsubscribe from marketing emails. You'll be amazed at how you can reduce the flow into your inbox with such a simple move, allowing you to focus on the messages that count. When you're in control it will allow you to feel positive rather than overwhelmed.

Always assume the best about someone and try to look for positive intentions behind actions. This way you're always focusing on the good things instead of the negatives.

november

Learn to knit. Doing something creative with your hands will take your mind off any problems and relax you as you focus on picking up a new skill. Best of all you'll have a lovely blanket or scarf you can keep or gift.

There is no way to be perfect and no fun in being perfect.

ALICIA KEYS

Book a day off work to spend time on yourself. It doesn't matter if you spend it on the sofa, shopping or at the cinema, just make sure you're doing something for yourself.

Start a positivity journal to record your thoughts and gratitudes. Make a list of things you're feeling grateful for and also a space for a "brain dump" where you can get out any random thoughts, making yourself feel lighter and ready for the day ahead.

Rearrange your furniture for a quick psychological boost. Even changing the pictures on your walls can help you see things differently.

06

For every minute you are angry, you lose sixty seconds of happiness.

RALPH WALDO EMERSON

If you're in the mood for a catch-up but leaving the house seems too much like hard work, book in a Zoom or Skype call with a friend.

••• (08) •••

If there's something that's been weighing on your mind, sit down and work out the steps you need to take to make the situation better, because even having a plan in place can make things seem more manageable.

••• (09) •••

Have something to look forward to after a hard day. It could be a glass of wine with friends, a trip to see a film or your favourite takeaway.

••• (10) •••

Match your music to your mood. If you're feeling excited and energetic, put on a pop song; if you're feeling melancholy, put on a "sad" song which you may find comforting and beautiful, resulting in you feeling more positive.

••• •••

Staying positive can often be a challenge, especially during the winter. Try reading an inspirational book with strong role models to help you change the way you see things.

••• •••

Give yourself a reason to get outside by getting something new to wear. It could be a bright hat with an oversized bobble, a cozy scarf or a new pair of boots. Whatever you choose, you'll be so keen to try it out that cold weather and grey skies won't stop you adventuring.

Success is getting what you want, happiness is wanting what you get.

W. P. KINSELLA

Create a positivity playlist. This way you'll have some mood-boosting songs at the touch of a button to listen to whenever you feel like you need a top-up of positivity.

If you're going out for dinner, add a little extra to your tip. You probably won't notice the money, but it could make a big difference to the restaurant staff. It will give you a lovely feeling to go with your full stomach.

••• •••

Be curious and approach the day by asking what you can learn from it. Positive people never stop learning and growing.

••• 17 •••

For a positive outcome, it's important to stay focused on your goals. Try not to let inconveniences in your present knock you off track. Break your tasks down into little steps so you can feel regular boosts as you achieve each one.

••• 18 •••

Make the most of dark evenings and light a sparkler. The fizzing flame will lift your spirits as you scribe and draw on the night sky canvas.

19

I firmly believe that when I am positive, it not only makes me better, but it also makes those around me better.

HARVEY MACKAY

Life isn't always easy. Sometimes things will crop up to create a bump in your path, but that's okay. By looking at the positives in your situation, you'll be able to learn, grow and keep moving forward — which is what life is all about.

Be yourself — it's the secret to happiness. Make a list of all your good and bad points and make a pledge to yourself to love them all.

Set yourself up for tomorrow morning by preparing your bag tonight. Know where your keys, wallet and phone all are and check the weather forecast to see if you need a coat or umbrella. This way you'll be able to leave on time and keep calm — a positive way to start your day!

••• 23 •••

Designate some time to surf the internet, but don't let yourself get sucked in for too long. To avoid wasting hours, set an alarm and then click away, guilt-free.

Practise the tightening and relaxing of your muscles so you learn to recognize tension and tightness and you'll be able to relax more easily. Start with your forehead and move slowly down to your toes, tightening and releasing each muscle group in turn. As you become used to the process, you should feel relaxation sweeping your body and when you're relaxed you will feel uplifted and positive.

Surround yourself with positive people, not the kind who are negative and jealous of everything you do.

HEIDI KLUM

• • ● (26) ● • •

Download a stargazing app on your phone and see
which constellations you can spot in the sky. It will
also help you gain perspective on any problems
that are feeling large in your life.

• • ● (27) ● • •

Use your fingertips to apply pressure to the space
between the knuckles of your index and middle
finger. Squeeze and then let go. This yoga-based
technique should help to create a state of calm.

• • ● (28) ● • •

Schedule a ten-minute worry window into your
day to deal with any concerns. Write them in a
notebook and leave them until the designated time.
When you know you have a strategy to handle your
worries, life feels more positive.

Be your best friend and give yourself a break. When you start to think about things negatively ask yourself what you would say to someone in the same position. Tell yourself you've got this!

Love your leftovers and make a big effort to reduce food waste. There are plenty of great ways to use up scraps such as making tea from apple cores or crisps from root veg peelings. You'll feel deeply satisfied knowing you haven't wasted anything.

december

01

Why not find a new activity to enjoy in the holiday season this year? Create some new traditions such as a wintry walk with hot chocolate or a day volunteering.

02

You can, you should, and if you're brave enough to start, you will.

STEPHEN KING

Get puzzling over a jigsaw puzzle — the harder the better. You can do it alone or with friends, but either way you'll find a huge sense of satisfaction when you complete it.

Turn off the mains and light some candles. Watching the soft flickering light and shadows the flames create is calming, allowing your thoughts to relax and drift.

•• • 05 • ••

Challenge yourself to eat the rainbow one day. Can you find natural foods that match all seven colours? Look how pretty they are on your plate and enjoy the fact they are healthy, too.

If you hold yourself to impossibly high standards, you'll always find yourself lacking. Instead, be kind to yourself and focus on the areas where you are happy and see what skills you have. Soon you'll see these grow in number and you'll be more positive about other things too.

Why not try and see positive things, to just touch those things and make them bloom?

THÍCH NHẤT HẠNH

Try doing a Sudoku or crossword. Your mind will feel exercised and more relaxed despite all the concentrating you have to do. It's like a physical workout for your brain.

Apply a face mask. Mash up a banana or avocado and apply liberally to your face. Shut your eyes and cover with slices of cucumber, if you have some. Relax and then wash off with warm water for glowing, soft skin.

••• (10) •••

Look back over the past year and reflect on positive things and your achievements.

••• (11) •••

Why not take some time to examine your life and note the things that don't cost money and bring you joy? You'll likely discover that happiness can't be bought in a shop.

••• (12) •••

Set up an obstacle course either outside or inside your home. Put cushions on the floor and place tables and chairs to climb over, under and through. Time yourself and any friends and family you can rope in.

Optimism is the most important human trait, because it allows us to evolve our ideas, to improve our situation, and to hope for a better tomorrow.

SETH GODIN

If organization brings you joy, put your bookshelves in order — choose whether you want them in order of author, subject or even spine colour.

Grow your own gifts such as drying herbs from your garden or taking a cutting and allowing it to propagate before potting it up and decorating with a ribbon. You'll feel a sense of achievement and the person who receives it will know it was grown with love.

Tap into aromatherapy by investing in wax melts and a burner. Then play around with fragrances to see which suits your needs. Vanilla is calming while rose is known for boosting your mood.

Create a mission statement. It will help you define your purpose in life and what motivates your behaviour. Every time you're feeling a bit lost or directionless refer back to it.

••• (18) •••

The sun himself is weak when he first rises and gathers strength and courage as the day gets on.

CHARLES DICKENS

••• (19) •••

Customize some brown paper for the most unique wrapping material around. Use ribbons or pens to make each gift really stand out. When the recipient sees the effort you've gone to, it will make you both feel good.

••• (20) •••

Pick up the phone and call a friend instead of sending a text. Hearing someone's voice can create a massive endorphin boost.

••● (21) ●••

Don't feel pressure to buy expensive gifts but give time tokens instead, promising to garden, babysit or just go for a walk together. You'll be amazed how well these are received.

••● (22) ●••

Treat yourself to an early night. It doesn't matter how early, simply draw the curtains, put on your coziest PJs, grab a book and jump under the covers.

••● (23) ●••

Learn to appreciate the little things in life. It might be watching a beautiful sunset, discovering some spare coins in your pocket or even catching a green light instead of being stuck at a red. Noticing them will add up throughout your day.

●●● ●●●

Remember that you're not defined by your success; every step you take toward your goal also counts.

●●● 25 ●●●

Try writing a song or poem. Sometimes the act of boiling down thoughts or feelings into just a few words or a chorus to be repeated helps you to get to the heart of the matter.

●●● 26 ●●●

You might not be able to get outside so a good alternative is to watch a nature documentary. Not only are they soothing, but they will also help you dream of adventures and highlight the scale of the natural world, which will allow you to gain perspective.

27

A problem is a chance for you to do your best.

DUKE ELLINGTON

Reboot your inner monologue and say the phrase: "I am not my thoughts; I am my actions" to yourself each morning. By realizing you're in control of your destiny you'll feel more positive.

●●● ●●●

Give yourself permission to say no. You don't have to go to parties or restaurants when you don't feel like it. Friends will understand if you'd rather skip a night out and there is joy to be found in doing what pleases you rather than others.

●●● (30) ●●●

Instead of batting away positive comments, learn how to accept a compliment. When you listen to others say good things about you and say thank you, you will start to believe them and really focus on those good qualities.

●●● (31) ●●●

Learn to be brave and take risks. Positive people take a chance, even if they are scared.

conclusion

Hopefully reading this book will have shown you there is not one way to live a positive life. Instead there are lots of little things you can do each day to ensure you notice the good in life rather than the bad. As you practise these positive habits, you'll soon learn that happiness is an attitude, not a situation. All you need to do is start with small steps and soon your journey on the path to positivity will be effortless. There are lots of fun activities that you can do to bring joy into your days. So fill your cup with these small moments and soon you'll find it's spilling over with positivity.

notes

....
....
....
....
....
....
....
....
....
....
....
....
....